WORLD OF WELLNESS
Health Education Series

WOW!
Ruby Explores the
World of Wellness

Student Book • Yellow Level

Bonnie K. Nygard
Tammy L. Green
Susan C. Koonce

Human Kinetics

Library of Congress Cataloging-in-Publication Data

Nygard, Bonnie.
    WOW! Ruby explores the world of wellness. Student book—yellow level / Bonnie K. Nygard,
Tammy L. Green, Susan C. Koonce.
            p. cm. -- (World of wellness health education series)
        Student text to: WOW! health education teacher's guide. Yellow level.
        ISBN 0-7360-5577-0 (soft cover)
        1. Health--Study and teaching (Elementary) I. Title: Ruby explores the world of wellness.
II. Green, Tammy. III. Koonce, Susan. IV. Nygard, Bonnie. WOW! health education teacher's guide.
Yellow level. V. Title. VI. Series.
        LB1587.A3N94 2005
        372.37--dc22

                                                                        2004024046

ISBN-10: 0-7360-5577-0 (soft cover); ISBN-10: 0-7360-6229-7 (hard cover)
ISBN-13: 978-0-7360-5577-2 (soft cover); ISBN-13: 978-0-7360-6229-9 (hard cover)

Acquisitions Editor: Bonnie Pettifor
Developmental Editor: Amy Stahl
Assistant Editor: Bethany J. Bentley
Copyeditor: Karen Bojda
Proofreader: Pam Johnson
Graphic Designer (Interior and Cover): Robert Reuther
Graphic Artist: Robert Reuther
Photo Manager: Kelly J. Huff
Photographer: Van Clifton
Art Manager: Kelly Hendren
Illustrators: Jenny L. Parum (cartoons) and Roberta Polfus (medical art)
Printer: Custom Color Graphics

Printed in the United States of America
10 9 8 7 6 5 4 3 2

Human Kinetics
Web site: www.HumanKinetics.com

United States: Human Kinetics
P.O. Box 5076
Champaign, IL 61825-5076
800-747-4457
e-mail: humank@hkusa.com

Canada: Human Kinetics
475 Devonshire Road Unit 100
Windsor, ON N8Y 2L5
800-465-7301 (in Canada only)
e-mail: orders@hkcanada.com

Europe: Human Kinetics
107 Bradford Road
Stanningley
Leeds LS28 6AT, United Kingdom
+44 (0) 113 255 5665
e-mail: hk@hkeurope.com

Australia: Human Kinetics
57A Price Avenue
Lower Mitcham, South Australia 5062
08 8277 1555
e-mail: liaw@hkaustralia.com

New Zealand: Human Kinetics
Division of Sports Distributors NZ Ltd.
P.O. Box 300 226 Albany
North Shore City
Auckland
0064 9 448 1207
e-mail: info@humankinetics.co.nz

Contents

Safety, Injury Prevention, Personal Health, and Physical Activity

1 Meet Ruby's Family

Today is the biggest,
scariest day of my life.
I can't wait!

Hi! My name is Ruby.
I like soccer, dancing,
and playing make-believe.

I also like dogs.
I wish I had a dog.

Not All Families Are Alike

Some families have . . .

▶ moms and dads.
▶ moms or dads.
▶ grandparents.
▶ brothers and sisters.
▶ aunts and uncles.
▶ friends.

All families care about each other!

Today is very busy at my house.
It is the first day of school.
My sister, Sydney, is helping put my hair in pretty purple ponytails.
Purple is my favorite color.
What's your favorite color?

Sydney is the oldest. She helps Mom and Dad take care of us.

My brother T.J. says Sydney is bossy.
He even made up a comic strip about Sydney.
He called it Bossy Belusa.
I don't think Sydney liked that comic strip.

My other brother, Cody, is excited about starting school.
He loves reading and learning and stuff.
I think I do too.

After breakfast, Mom told us to sit on the couch so she could take a "first day of school" picture. She said, "Hold up the number of fingers to show what grade you are starting today."

I held up one finger.
Cody held up three fingers.
T.J. held up four fingers.
Sydney held up five fingers.

Can you tell what grades we are starting today?

How many fingers is Ruby holding up?
Hop forward that many times.

How many fingers is Cody holding up?
Jump sideways that many times.

How many fingers is T.J. holding up?
Jog backward that many times.

How many fingers is Sydney holding up?
Leap forward that many times.

English and Swahili [swah-HEE-lee], which is also called Kiswahili [kee-swah-HEE-lee], are the official languages taught in the schools in Kenya, a country in Africa.

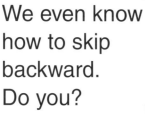

2 Who's a Stranger?

My older sister, Sydney, walks with me to school.
On our way, we pick up Neka. Neka is my best friend.

Do you want to know a secret?
Neka and I never walk! We skip, gallop, jump, and leap all the way to school. We even know how to skip backward. Do you?

Sydney is serious about getting to school safely. We have to stick together. She says there might be a **stranger** along the way.

That is someone who I don't know.
Sydney told me not to talk to strangers.
She also told me never to get into a stranger's car.

I told Neka about stranger danger so she can stay safe from strangers too.

Stranger Safety

Do . . .

▶ Stick with a buddy.

▶ Ask your family before leaving your home.

▶ Say "no" in a loud voice if someone tries to take you somewhere or touch you in a way that makes you feel bad.

▶ Get away fast and go to a safe place if a stranger follows you.

Do Not . . .

▶ Get into a stranger's car.

▶ Go anywhere with a stranger.

▶ Open your door to a stranger.

▶ Tell your address to a stranger on the phone.

Then Neka asked, "What about **bullies?**"

Bullies are kids who are not very nice.

I told Neka that if someone is not nice to me, I ask them to stop.

If they don't stop, I tell an adult.

That usually does the trick.

What do you do when someone is not nice to you?

WOW! 'Em

W = Wait before reacting.

O = Organize a plan (think of different ways to handle the problem).

W = Walk away if you can't agree without losing tempers.

How far can you jump? Bend your knees and swing your arms forward as you jump. When you land, bend your knees again. Wow!

Emus [EE-myooz] cannot walk backward.

Shrimp can only swim backward.

WOW! Ruby Explores the World of Wellness • Yellow Level • UNIT 1—Lesson 2: Who's a Stranger?

5

3 Secret Safety Codes

My brother Cody is super smart. On our way to school, Cody taught Neka and me a secret safety code for crossing the street.

It goes like this . . .

Look left, look right.
Make sure no car is in sight.
Look left one more time
To finish this safety rhyme!

If no car is coming, we can cross the street.
It works and it's fun!

Neka and I made up our own secret safety codes.

They go like this . . .

Hop in and
pull out the strap.
Now buckle it
across your lap!

Bike, Walk, or Ride

Bike Safety Tips

- Ride your bike with traffic.
- Wear a helmet.
- Wear bright clothing.
- Use proper hand signals.
- Walk—do not ride—your bike across the street.

Walking to School Safety Tips

- Try *not* to walk alone.
- Watch out for cars.
- Look both ways twice before crossing the street.

Bus Safety Tips

- Do *not* move around in the bus.
- Talk quietly. Do not yell in the bus.
- Wear a seat belt in a car.

Put on a helmet, nice and tight, And wear clothes that are super bright. Use your hand to make a turn, 'Cause safety rules are fun to learn!

Can you guess what our secret safety codes are for?

4 Shaking, Spinning, and Blowing

Ms. Ling is my first-grade teacher. I like my new teacher.

Ms. Ling taught us the "be safe at school" rules. She said to stay away from windows if there is an earthquake. We practiced hiding under our desks and in doorways. That was cool.

We got to go under our desks two more times. That was when we pretended there was a hurricane and tornado. Neka and I were always the quickest! No pointy pieces of glass would ever catch us.

R-R-Ring! Fire Drill!

▶ Listen to your teacher.
▶ Walk—do not run.
▶ Exit the building.

Earthquake Safety

▶ Indoors—Stand in a doorway.
▶ Outdoors—Stay away from buildings, trees, and power lines.

Hurricane Safety

▶ Look for shelter.
▶ Stay out of low areas because heavy rain may cause a flood.

The part I liked best was the pretend fire drill. We got to go outside. But we had to be quiet and come right back in. Next time I think they should let us take recess since we're already outside.

I would go right to the swings.

What do you like to do at recess?

What do cows do after an earthquake?

Tornado Safety

▶ Indoors—Stay away from windows.
▶ Outdoors—Look for shelter in a sturdy building, but not a trailer. If there is no shelter, lie down in a ditch and cover your head with your hands.

Winter Storm Safety

▶ Stay indoors.
▶ If you have to go outdoors, wear layers of warm clothing.

Heat and Sun Safety

▶ Wear sunscreen.
▶ Wear a hat.
▶ Drink water.
▶ Stay in the shade.

5 Scrub a Dub Dub

Washing hands is a big deal at school.

Ms. Ling let us put glitter all over our hands.
We pretended the glitter was **germs.**

Then we washed our hands the regular way.
Kids that didn't use soap still had glitter on their hands.
Some kids had glitter between their fingers.

Do you wash between your fingers?

If we don't use soap and scrub all over our hands, some of the germs will stick. Neka and I decided to always use soap.

We think germs are gross.

Pretend you are a soap bubble swirling through the air. Pop!

In Japan, people wash before they get into the bath.

Washing Hands Is a *Big* Deal!

How to Wash Your Hands

▶ Wet hands with warm water.

▶ Add soap and rub hands together, front side, back side, and in between.

▶ Rinse hands with warm water.

▶ Dry hands—every drop!

When to Wash Your Hands

▶ Before you eat or touch food

▶ After using the restroom

▶ After playing outside

▶ After sneezing

▶ After touching something a sick person has touched

6

My New Purple Toothbrush

Guess what!
I lost two of my bottom teeth.
My top tooth is wiggly.
T.J. wants to pull it out, but I won't let him.

Last week my dad took us to the **dentist.**
My stomach had the flip-flops. But the
dentist was nice!

Brush away dog breath!

The dentist told me about
brushing.
Now I brush every single
tooth.

T.J. had a hole in his tooth.
The dentist called it a **cavity.**
She told T.J. to brush better
and eat less candy.

I bet the candy part is going
to be hard.

Four Steps to Healthy Teeth

1. Brush your teeth two times a day.
2. Floss between your teeth every day.
3. Eat healthy foods.
4. Visit your dentist.

Good for Your Teeth

Calcium-rich foods like milk, cheese, and yogurt.

Not Good for Your Teeth

Sugary, sticky foods like soda, candy, cookies, and fruit roll-ups.

Children in many countries receive money and small gifts from the Tooth Fairy for lost baby teeth. Spanish children are visited by Perez, the Little Mouse.

7 Heart Healthy

One of my favorite parts of school is called recess. Recess has rules too! We have to take turns and never push other kids. Those rules are so we won't get hurt or in trouble.

My two favorite things to do at recess are called "swing" and "tag."

Swinging is like flying. Playing tag is running in different directions. That is so "It" won't catch me. Running makes my heart beat faster.

Did you know that your **heart** is a **muscle**?

Ms. Ling told us to run off our steam at recess. She says it will make all of our muscles sturdy and strong.
I think it's so we won't have any steam left to jiggle in our seats.

Cody told me that caterpillars have more than 2,000 muscles.
I think it's because they have so many legs to move.
I wonder if they keep all those muscles when they turn into butterflies.

Mexican folk music is called son [SOAN], which means sound. Son is played on guitars and a harp or violin for a foot-stamping dance.

Being Active . . .

▶ Is fun.
▶ Helps you forget your problems.
▶ Is healthy for your body.
▶ Makes your muscles stronger.
▶ Makes your heart and lungs stronger.
▶ Helps you sleep better.

Happy Heart Activities!

▶ Bike riding
▶ Playing tag
▶ Swimming
▶ Playing soccer or basketball
▶ Skating

What other activities make your heart smile? Pretend to do your favorite activity!

Recess Rules!

⬤ Have fun and keep moving!
⬤ Wait your turn for equipment.
⬤ Do *not* push or fight.

ZZZZZ—Getting Enough Sleep Is Important

▶ You will have more energy during the day.
▶ You will be ready to learn.
▶ You will be in a better mood, which makes your friends, family, and teacher happy!

You should get 10 to 11 hours of sleep every night.

8

Sturdy, Strong, and Stretchy

My family sure is on the go!
I play soccer.
Cody plays baseball.
T.J. plays basketball.
Sydney plays hockey.
We have balls, bats, and
skates all over our house.

Guess what!
My dad is my soccer coach.
I call him "Coach Dad."
The other kids just call him
"Coach."

Soccer sure has a lot of running.
Coach Dad said running will make my heart muscle stronger.

I think soccer also makes my leg muscles stronger.
My legs have to run, kick, and dribble the ball.
Legs must have a lot of different muscles.

Muscles can also reach in different directions.
Coach Dad taught us a bunch of different ways to stretch our muscles.
Are your muscles sturdy, strong, and stretchy?

A box turtle can carry up to 200 times its own weight on its shell. For a human, this would be like lifting three elephants.

Thumpity-Thump! Rules for Heart-Healthy Activity

- Your heart beats faster than normal but ○ not too fast.
- You breathe harder than normal but ○ not too hard.

Is soccer a heart-healthy activity? Why?

Sturdy, Strong, and Stretchy Muscles

▶ Move-move-moving your muscles will make them strong so they don't get tired when working a long time. This is **muscular endurance.**

▶ Stretch-stretch-stretching your muscles will make them flexible. This is **flexibility.**

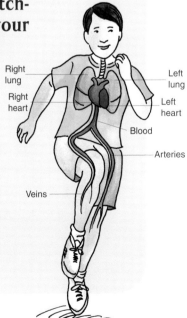

Right lung

Right heart

Left lung

Left heart

Blood

Arteries

Veins

9 Family Fitness Fun

"Sharing time" is fun.
One day, Ms. Ling asked us
to share the different **verbs**
we do with our family.

Neka said she rides
bikes with her mom.
Some kids go hiking
or fly kites.
One kid walks his dog
with his grandpa.

I wish I had a dog.

Finally, it was my turn
to share!
I said that my family
goes swimming together.
I don't even have to wear
a lifejacket . . . when my
mom or dad is near.
My swimsuit is pretty.

Last summer, my mom bought special sunscreen that stays on in the water. That way I could play in the sun without getting burned. My brother T.J. didn't wear sunscreen, and his skin turned red-red-red. He couldn't go swimming for two whole days. He was mad-mad-mad!

Neka and I made up a secret safety code for the pool.

It goes like this . . .

Put on sunscreen
so you don't burn,
And before jumping in,
take your turn.
Walk on deck and
do not run,
So your time at the
pool is fun-fun-fun!

Physical Activity and Family Fitness Fun!

▶ Take a walk.

▶ Dance in your living room.

▶ Play tag.

▶ Fly a kite.

▶ Ride bikes.

▶ Go swimming together.

Pool and Sun Safety

● Do learn how to swim.

● Do not swim alone.

● Do wear sunscreen, even if your skin is already brown.

● Do not run on deck.

 How do baby fish swim?

10 The Quick Creepy Crawl

My big sister, Sydney,
is learning how to be a
babysitter.
She lets me practice safety
stuff with her.

Like if there is a fire, would
you know what to do?
Sydney says that if we see
smoke, we have to leave the
house in a jiffy.

If there is a lot of smoke, we have to do the quick creepy crawl.

The most important thing is to get out of the house. Then we used my pretend cell phone to call **911.**

If your clothes catch on fire . . .

1. *Stop.*

2. *Drop* to the ground.

3. *Roll* over and over.

Fire Safety

▶ Get out of the house.

▶ If smoke is in the air, crawl under the smoke.

▶ After you are out, call 911 for help!

Practice the quick creepy crawl!

Calling 911

▶ Tell them who you are.

▶ Know the address and phone number of where you are during the emergency.

▶ Tell them what happened.

▶ Stay on the phone until they say to hang up.

11 Don't Be Tricked

Sydney taught me about **phone safety.** She said to never let a stranger know when an adult is not home.

It's pretty easy.
I just say that my mom and dad can't come to the phone.
Then I ask if I can take a message.

Sydney says if someone makes me feel squirmy inside, I can hang up.
Just like that.

Sydney said I'm supposed to tell an adult if someone makes me feel squirmy inside.
No matter what!

There are a lot of ways to be tricked. Sometimes medicine looks like candy, but it's not.

 Sometimes **poison** looks safe to drink, but it's not. Some guns look like toys, but they're not. You have to be careful or you could be tricked.

Neka tried to pet a dog on the way to school. When she got close, he growled and showed his teeth. Neka almost got tricked.

Good Touch, Bad Touch

- Your body is special and private.
- Do *not* let anyone touch you on your private body parts.
- Do tell an adult if someone makes you feel bad by touching you.

After that, Sydney made us walk on the other side of the street.

If I had a dog, it would be nice. I wish I had a dog.

Choices

 Do . . .

▶ Wear sunscreen.
▶ Talk about disagreements.
▶ Ask before leaving your home.
▶ Get along with others.
▶ Be active.

 Do Not . . .

▶ Swim alone.
▶ Fight.
▶ Go with a stranger.
▶ Be a bully.
▶ Be a couch or mouse potato (someone who sits and plays with electronic games or watches TV too much).

Nutrition Education

12 Food for Thought

You won't believe all the stuff
I do *before* school starts!
I make my bed, get dressed,
pack my backpack, eat
breakfast, and brush my
teeth.
Being in first grade
is a lot of work!

Mom says I have to eat a
healthy breakfast, stuff like
oatmeal and cereal.
She also makes sure
I eat fruit every day.
My yummiest fruits are
bananas and grapes.
What do you eat for
breakfast?

Ms. Ling says that eating breakfast will make my brain think better.
I don't know why, because food goes to my **stomach.**

Ms. Ling says that my body also needs water. She calls it **hydration** [high-DRAY-shun]. I think it's so my body doesn't dry up.
It's a good thing I like water. Do you?

Scottish people eat porridge. You probably call it oatmeal.

Japanese people start their day with miso soup, a soy broth with rice.

Eat a Healthy Breakfast!

▶ It gives you energy to go.
▶ It gives you **nutrients** to learn.

Breakfast Brain Boosters!

▶ Oatmeal and fruit
▶ Whole-grain cereal and low-fat milk
▶ Whole-grain toast and peanut butter
▶ Flour tortilla and fruit
▶ Miso [MEE-so] soup
▶ Yogurt and fruit

Gulp, Gulp

▶ Drink water every day.
▶ Drink water before and after you are active.
▶ Drink extra water in hot weather.
▶ Drink water even if you're not thirsty!

13   A Crunch for Lunch

I help my mom pack
healthy stuff for lunch.
First I have to wash
my hands.
Then I have to wash my
grapes so I won't eat **germs.**

Sometimes Cody helps
me make my lunch.
He adds carrots and celery.
I like grapes better. Grapes
are purple.

Sydney makes the best sandwiches.
She calls them nutty banana sandwiches.
They're made with peanut butter and bananas. Yum!

T.J. is the best snack packer.
He packs stuff like granola bars, tortillas, or applesauce.

I drink milk at school.
Drinking milk will help me grow strong bones.

What do you crunch and munch for lunch?

Food Safety Rules

- Do wash your hands before touching food.
- Do *not* eat food that has been left out in the sun or heat.
- Do keep food refrigerated.
- Do *not* accept food from a stranger.
- Do wash fruits and vegetables before eating.

Healthy Snacks!

▶ Apple
▶ Granola bar
▶ Celery sticks
▶ Rice cakes
▶ Yogurt smoothie
▶ Water, water, water!

Because It's Good for You!

 Water is good for your whole body!

 Whole grains give you energy!

 Fruits give you energy and a healthy body!

 Vegetables give you energy and a healthy body!

 Low-fat protein helps build muscles!

 Calcium gives you healthy bones and teeth!

In China, rice is usually eaten with every meal.

14   Tacos by Cody

Last night Cody made
dinner at our house.
He called his dinner
Tacos by Cody.
He said that dinner
was his homework.
I can't wait until
I'm in third grade.
Their homework
sounds like fun!

Cody's friend, Juan, didn't
make dinner for his family.
Instead, Juan's family went to
Tasty Tillies!
Yes, third grade sure does
sound like fun!

Juan told everyone in his
family what they could order.
"No extra-larging allowed!"
Juan said.
His family ordered soup,
salad, and baked potatoes.

What Does Your Family Eat?

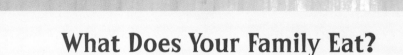

Potatoes	Bananas	Carrots	Chicken	Yogurt
Rice	Mangoes	Peas	Beans	Cheese
Tortillas	Apples	Lettuce	Pork	Milk

I didn't know that Tasty Tillies had salad.
Did you?

In Belgium, fried potatoes are a favorite snack.

Make Healthy Choices at Fast-Food Restaurants!

High-Calorie, High-Fat, Fast-Food Choices

▶ Quarter-pound (110-gram) cheeseburger, large fries, and a 16-ounce (475-milliliter) soda

▶ Four slices of sausage and mushroom pizza and a 16-ounce (475-milliliter) soda

▶ Two pieces of fried chicken (breast and wing), buttermilk biscuit, mashed potatoes and gravy, corn on the cob, and a 16-ounce (475-milliliter) soda

Lower-Calorie, Less-Fat, Fast-Food Choices

▶ Hamburger, small fries, and a 16-ounce (475-milliliter) diet soda

▶ Three slices of cheese pizza with a 16-ounce (475-milliliter) diet soda

▶ One piece of fried chicken (wing), mashed potatoes and gravy, coleslaw, and a 16-ounce (475-milliliter) diet soda

15

Go-Go-Go!

"Snort-snort! Neigh!"
That is Neka and me
during soccer practice.
Today we're pretending
to be horses.
Sometimes we're monkeys,
grasshoppers, tigers, bears,
and other wild creatures.

Coach Dad is the best coach.
He lets us do all kinds of fun
stuff.
He also teaches us how to
play soccer sometimes.

Coach Dad told us to eat a healthy snack before practice.
He said that eating a healthy snack is like putting gas in a car.
It will help us go-go-go!

When Neka and I go-go-go, we run, **gallop, skip,** and **jump.**
Sometimes we hop like frogs.

Healthy foods give you long-lasting energy to go-go-go!

More Healthy Snacks!

▶ Low-fat tortilla chips and salsa
▶ Sunflower seeds
▶ Grapes
▶ Pretzels
▶ String cheese
▶ Carrot sticks
▶ Water, water, water!

Pretend to be a cloud that is full of water. Now become rain, sleet, or snow!

The most popular sport in the world is soccer. Soccer is known as football in some places around the world.

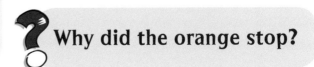

Why did the orange stop?

16

All Living Things

Today I was a seed in school.
When Neka watered me,
I started to grow into a plant.
When the sun came out,
I grew big-big-bigger.
The more Neka fed me,
the bigger I grew.

I was the biggest plant ever!

Ms. Ling said that we are
all living things.
We need food and water
to grow.

We feed a lot of things
at our house.
We feed our fish.
That is Sydney's job.
We feed our gerbil.
That is T.J.'s job.
We feed our plants.
That is Cody's job.
If we had a dog,
I would feed him.
I wish I had a dog.

Guess what!
Dad even feeds the grass!
He says sprinklers aren't
just for running through.
It's fun to help Dad with
his job.

What do you feed at your
house?

All Living Things Need Food!

▶ Plants
▶ Animals
▶ People
▶ Insects
▶ You

Why Do We Need Food?

▶ Health
▶ Energy
▶ Growth

Eating healthy and being active is *great!*

Prance, pounce, and plop!

People who live in Kenya eat mashed bananas, called matoke [mah-TOE-kay].

UNIT 3

Growth and Development, Body Systems, Health Promotion, and Disease Prevention

17 Big and Strong

I'm wearing new purple shoes today.
Mom says I'm going through a **growth spurt.**
That means my bones are getting longer.
I'm as tall as Cody. Well, almost.

I'm taller than Neka—that is for sure.
Neka is eating super-duper, grow-fast food.
She's also walking her dog every single day.
I think she's trying to catch up.

I wish I had a dog.

Growing Taller, Stronger, and Bigger

 Do . . .

▶ Eat healthy foods.

▶ Drink water.

▶ Move your body.

 Do Not . . .

▶ Eat foods with a lot of fat and sugar.

▶ Drink a lot of soda.

▶ Be a couch or mouse potato. What do you think a mouse potato is?

18 Busy Body

Today, Ms. Ling taught us about how our bodies work. Our bodies sure are busy.

My **brain** helps me think.

My **lungs** help me breathe.

My **stomach** helps me digest my food.

My **skin** protects my insides.

My **blood** carries food to my muscles.

And my most magnificent, mighty **muscle** is my **heart.**

Coach Dad says that running
is good for my heart.
When I run, my heart goes
thumpity-thump.

What is your most
magnificent, mighty muscle?

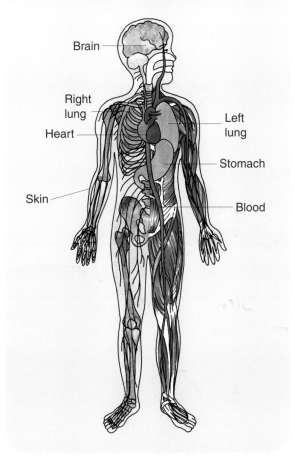

How Busy Is Your Body?

Brain

Right lung

Heart

Left lung

Stomach

Skin

Blood

In Japan, slices of fresh fruit are served at the end of a meal for dessert.

What does a moose get when he lifts weights?

Be a Busy Body!

▶ Walk a dog.
▶ Go bowling.
▶ Go canoeing.
▶ Plant a garden.
▶ Play a sport.

19

Cinco Senses

Ms. Ling taught us a rhyme called "Cinco Senses."

It goes like this . . .

Uno *tongue is for taste.*
Uno *nose is to smell.*
Dos *ears are to hear*
The ringing school bell.

Diez *fingers and toes*
Help me to touch.
Dos *eyes are for seeing*
Oh so much.

Do you know what *cinco* means?

Shake, rattle, and jiggle
different parts of your body!

Making Sense of Senses

▶ Eyes—Seeing
▶ Ears—Hearing
▶ Skin—Touching
▶ Tongue—Tasting
▶ Nose—Smelling

Can you count to 10 in Spanish?

1	**Uno** [U-no]	6	**Seis** [SACE]
2	**Dos** [DOS]	7	**Siete** [see-YAY-tay]
3	**Tres** [TRACE]	8	**Ocho** [OH-cho]
4	**Cuatro** [KWA-tro]	9	**Nueve** [new-WEH-vay]
5	**Cinco** [SING-ko]	10	**Diez** [dee-ACE]

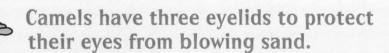

Camels have three eyelids to protect their eyes from blowing sand.

A dolphin can hear underwater sound from 15 miles (24 kilometers) away.

Tigers have striped skin, not just striped fur.

What part of your body has the most rhythm?

20 Glasses Can Be Cool

Mom says she wears **glasses**
because they help her see things better,
near and far.
I hope I get real glasses some day.
I think glasses are cool.

My grandpa wears a thing
in his ear.
It's called a **hearing aid.**
He says it helps him hear
better, loud and clear.
I wonder how that teeny-tiny
hearing aid works.
Do you know?

Glasses Are Cool!

▶ Glasses can help you see
far-away things.

▶ Glasses can help you see
near or small things.

Hearing Is Cool Too!

▶ If you have trouble
hearing, see a doctor.

▶ You may need a hearing
aid.

Can you gallop backward?
Give it a try!

A chameleon [kuh-MEEL-yun] can
look forward and backward at the
same time. Each of its eyes can
swivel in all directions all by itself.

21 Being Sick Is Boring

When I grow up, I want to be a doctor.
I'll get to look in kids' eyes and ears
with a teeny-tiny flashlight.
That part is more fun than the shot part.
Dr. Carter said I have to get shots
so I won't get sick.
I think I like shots better than getting sick.

Dr. Carter told me to eat
lots of fruits and vegetables,
drink water, wash my hands,
and exercise.
That way I'll be in tip-top
shape to play with my friends.

Being sick is boring.
Being bored is annoying.

Saunter forward *cuatro*
steps, and then melt to the
floor!

Who Do You See . . .

▶ If you are sick? A doctor
or a nurse

▶ If you have a toothache? A
dentist

▶ To get your eyes checked?
An optometrist [op-TOM-
uh-trist]

▶ If you need to talk about
big problems? A counselor
[KOWN-suh-ler] or other
trained person who
counsels

An immunization [IM-yuh-
nuh-ZAY-shun] is a shot that
a doctor or nurse gives you
to help your body fight sickness and keep you well.

**What did the pony tell the doctor
when she had a sore throat?**

22   I Had a Bug in My Throat

Cody had to go to Dr. Carter when he had an earache. Mom said he couldn't share his **medicine** with me.

Medicine is only for when you're sick.

One time I had a bug in my throat, but it wasn't a real bug.
It was a sickness that was caused by germs.

Dad took me to Dr. Carter, and Dr. Carter gave me medicine too. My medicine didn't taste like bubblegum.

I sure was glad when my bug went away.

Follow the Medicine Rules

- ○ Only take medicine from a trusted adult.
- ● Do not share medicine or take someone else's medicine.

Things That Can Happen When You're Sick

Things that can happen	You might have . . .	You might need . . .
Runny nose, sneezing, and cough	Common cold	Rest, **fluids**
Headache and fever	Flu	Rest, fluids, medicine
Pink and scratchy eye	Pink eye	Medicine
Scratchy throat and cough	Sore throat	Rest, fluids, medicine
Pain in your ear	Ear infection	Rest, fluids, medicine
Itchy scalp	Lice	Medicine

Medicine is not for sharing. Physical activity is great for sharing. What is an activity you will do this week during recess?

Blowing your nose in public is frowned on in Japan.

23 Germs, Germs, Germs

Today Ms. Ling let us play make-believe.
We got to pretend we were **germs.**
Germs are tiny living things that
you can't even see.
We got to move all around the room.
Germs can be everywhere.

Nurse Debbie came to our class.
She taught us how to keep safe from germs.
We practiced sneezing and coughing into our elbows.

She also taught us a song that goes like this . . .

If you have to cough
or sneeze,
Use a tissue please,
please, please!

Nurse Debbie said it's okay to share books and crayons.
It's not okay to share toothbrushes, straws, or combs.

I guess germs really are everywhere.

Germs are also called pathogens [PATH-uh-jenz].

How Germs Are Spread

▶ **Touching other people**
▶ **Through the air by coughing or sneezing**
▶ **Touching things that a sick person has touched**
▶ **Through some insects, such as flies or mosquitoes**

Pretend to be a pathogen twirling through the air after someone has sneezed.

People in Thailand think of the left hand as unclean, so they do not eat with it.

Mental, Emotional, Family, and Social Health

24 What Is a Family?

Today we drew pictures of our **families.**
We put all of our pictures on the wall.
They all look different.

Some kids
don't have
any brothers
and sisters.

Different Kinds of Families

▶ A mother, a father, and one child or more

▶ One parent and one child or more

▶ Two adults

▶ A parent and a stepparent and one child or more

▶ Grandparents or aunts or uncles and cousins

Some kids have babies
in their families.
I wish we had a baby—
and a dog.

My sister, Sydney, looks
different from the rest of us.
She's **adopted.**
That means my parents
picked her when she
was a baby.
They didn't get to pick me.

Have some active fun with
your family by creating one
of the following games!

▶ "Sturdy and Strong" game
▶ "Heart Happy" game
▶ "Mighty Muscle" game

What do you think each of
these games would be like?

What Makes You Unique?

▶ How tall or short you are
▶ If you have curly or straight hair
▶ The color of your skin, hair, and eyes
▶ What kind of family you have
▶ Your background and traditions

What else makes you unique?

How Are Most People Alike?

▶ They need food and a place to live.
▶ They want to be safe and loved.
▶ They like feeling good about themselves.

What else do you like?

25 The Family Meeting

My mom and dad say families should help each other.
Sometimes that means doing **chores.** Other times it means not fighting.

But what I like best is when we do fun stuff together—like going on picnics, swimming, or bike rides.

The part about not fighting is hard.

Sometimes Sydney is grumpy. She says I follow her around too much.
T.J. gets cranky when Cody messes with his comic books.

When we get mad at each other, we have a family meeting.
That is when we sit at the kitchen table and talk.
We mostly talk about why we got mad.
I like family meetings.

Do you have family meetings at your house?

Family Fun

▶ Play games.
▶ Talk.
▶ Share.
▶ Take care of each other.
▶ Be active together.

Family Activities

▶ Walk together.
▶ Dance together.
▶ Play together.
▶ Ride bikes together.
▶ Ski together.
▶ Paddle a canoe together.

Ruby says she has to do chores. What are chores? What kinds of things do you do to help your family?

Boys from the Maasai [mah-SIGH] tribe (in Kenya, a country in Africa) become warriors (called moran) when they are 14 years old.

 What clothing does a house wear?

26

Sad, Mad, Glad

Ms. Ling says when we are feeling **sad,** we should talk to her.
Neka's cat died, and she was sad. She cried and cried.

Ms. Ling told her it was okay to be sad.
I sure would be sad if I had a dog that died.
I wish I had a dog.

Sometimes kids get **mad**
at school.
Ms. Ling taught us things
to do when we get mad.
She said to take big breaths
and never hit anyone.
I think madness or sadness
can become **gladness**
when you talk about it.

What do you think?

Emotions

- Angry
- Sad
- Frustrated
- Glad
- Happy
- Excited

Talk About Your Feelings

- You will feel better.
- You will make a decision about how to deal with what is making you sad or mad.

Be Active to Deal With Emotions!

- Sprint.
- Play Frisbee with a friend.
- Go in-line skating.
- Dodge, dance, and dash.

27

The Cheetah and the Antelope

I crept quietly through the living room and into the bedroom.
I knew the cheetah [CHEE-tuh] was close.
If I wasn't careful, he would pounce out of the shadows and catch me.

That is when T.J. shouted, "Watch out, Ruby!"
I screamed and darted out of the room.

Boy, was Cody mad! He was the cheetah who was hunting me.

Cody said that T.J. ruined
our game.

Mom called a family meeting.
She said, "No yelling."
That was hard for Cody.
He wanted to yell at T.J.

Cody and T.J. got to talk
about what happened.
They also got to talk about
how it made them feel.
T.J. was sorry because
he wrecked our game.
Mom told him he should
show more **respect** next
time.

Do you know what *respect*
means?

After that, Cody wasn't mad
anymore.
He snuck out of the room
to find a new hiding place.
I bounded down the
stairs like a real antelope
[ANT-uh-lope].

Game on!

Respect!

▶ **Be a good listener.**

▶ **Do not tease or be a bully.**

▶ **Share.**

▶ **Take your turn.**

▶ **Say "please" and "thank you."**

▶ **Do your own work.**

Dealing With Feelings

▶ **Mad: Take a deep breath.**

▶ **Sad: Talk to an adult.**

▶ **Frustrated: Talk about how you feel.**

Creep forward *cinco* steps,
and then pounce!

28 Who's Your Listening Friend?

Ms. Ling taught us about making good **choices.** When she reads a story, she tells us to sit next to a "listening friend."

That is someone who won't talk to me when I am supposed to be listening.

Sometimes I want to sit next to Neka.
I know I'll talk to her.
So I pick someone else.
That is making a good choice.

Neka is my best friend from kindergarten.
She likes to do a lot of the same things I do.
She plays soccer and rides her bike, and her favorite color is purple.
My mom says it's good to have lots of different friends.

Do you have different friends?

What Are Friends?

▶ Friends are loyal.
▶ Friends respect each other.
▶ Friends are interested in what you have to say.
▶ Friends are fun to play with.

Make a Good Decision

1. Think about your decision before acting.
2. Think about all the different things that could happen.
3. Think about how your family would feel about your decision.
4. Make your decision.
5. Think about your decision.
6. Think about how you could make a better decision next time.

Alcohol, Tobacco, and Other Drugs

-No way!

29

"No Way!"

I stood up and said, "No way!"
That is what I would say if someone
tried to give me a cigarette or a pill.
Ms. Ling says pills aren't always
medicine.

—No way!

They are sometimes bad **drugs** that can hurt you or even make you die.

Only doctors or an adult who you know and trust can give you medicine.

What would you say if someone else tried to give you medicine?

No way!

Say No

1. Say "no!" in a strong voice.
2. Say why not.
3. Suggest doing something else.
4. Walk away.

Drugs or Medicine

▶ Some people take harmful drugs to change their body or mind.

▶ Your doctor gives you medicine or you buy it at a store to help your body fight an illness.

30

Look-Alikes

T.J. was sick this week.
Dr. Carter gave him pretty
pink pills.
They looked just like candy,
but they weren't.

The bottle of pills had T.J.'s
name written on it.
Mom said that is because
they are only for T.J.

The bottle also said that
T.J. had to take two pills
every day.
Mom gave him one in the
morning and one before
he went to bed.

I asked what would happen
if T.J. took more than two pills
a day.
Mom said that T.J. could
get very sick if he took
too many pills.
Maybe he would even have
to go to the hospital!

I guess that is why Mom or
Dad is the boss of taking
medicine at our house.

**Sometimes drugs look like
candy, but drugs are *not*
candy!**

**Take medicine only if a
doctor or an adult you trust
gives it to you.**

**Taking medicine that is not
yours can make you sick!**

**Slide in a straight line, in
a zigzag pattern, and in a
curvy line.**

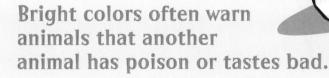

**Bright colors often warn
animals that another
animal has poison or tastes bad.**

31

Yuck!

Cigarettes stink! Yuck.

Cigarettes can make
you sick. The smoke hurts
your lungs.
I need my lungs so I can
play soccer, swim, and ride
my bike.

What do you need
your lungs for?

Alcohol and Drugs Can Hurt Your Body

1. Alcohol and drugs make it harder for you to make good decisions.
2. Alcohol and drugs damage your liver. The liver cleans up the waste in the body.
3. Alcohol can damage your heart.

Smoking Tobacco . . .

▶ Harms your lungs.
▶ Harms your heart.
▶ Can be addictive.

Chewing Tobacco . . .

▶ Can cause mouth or throat cancer.
▶ Harms your heart.
▶ Can be addictive.

Secondhand smoke does firsthand damage to your lungs and can cause asthma attacks or other illnesses.

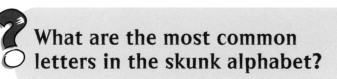

? What are the most common letters in the skunk alphabet?

32 Some Things Are Not for Kids

Mom and Dad said that alcohol
is a drug, too.
Alcohol is stuff like beer and wine.
Alcohol is not for kids.

Alcohol is also not good for adults if they drink too much. My uncle drank too much alcohol and had to go to a special hospital.
I don't think being in a hospital is fun.

Alcohol Abuse Can Lead to Big Problems

Alcohol Can . . .

▶ Cause problems with family and friends.

▶ Be addictive.

▶ Make doing everyday tasks harder.

▶ Make doing physical activity harder.

Can you balance on three body parts?

Community, Consumer, and Environmental Health

33 Taking Care of Each Other

Our class is a **community.**
We all work together.
Sometimes we help keep our classroom tidy.
We also take care of each other.
I like our class community.

My neighborhood is a community too.
When I get scared, I know just what houses to go to.
They'll always help me.
Do you have safe places where you live?

We also have **helpers** in our community, like police officers and firefighters. If we need help, we can call 911, and someone will come to help us.

Ms. Ling said that doctors and nurses help keep our community healthy.

Did you know that there are different kinds of doctors? Some doctors are for eyes. Some doctors are for teeth. Some doctors are for kids. Some doctors are for animals.

I wish I had a dog.

What Is a Community?

▶ Your classroom
▶ Your school
▶ Your neighborhood
▶ Your town or city
▶ Your state, country, and planet

Community Helpers

▶ Police officers
▶ Firefighters
▶ Emergency workers
▶ Doctors and nurses

Can you name other community helpers?

How many different ways can you stretch your body?

 Traditional Japanese people do not eat outside in public unless they have a place to sit down.

Help Out!

 Do . . .

▶ Help other people.
▶ Help keep your community clean.

Do Not . . .

▶ Do not fight or be a bully.
▶ Do not litter.

34   Only One Earth

I'm a helper in my community too.
Last week we did a neighborhood cleanup.
We picked up trash in big orange bags.

Mom said it was okay to pick up trash.
It was not okay to pick up sharp things.
I told my class all about it.

Then we talked about why we should never litter. That means throwing trash on the ground.

Ms. Ling says we live on an awesome planet. It's called **earth.**
Our solar system is gigantic. But there is only one earth. When you only have one of something, you have to take care of it.
If you don't, then you'll have none.

Earth has **land, water,** and **air**. There are laws to keep earth clean.
That is because all living things need clean air and water to live.

I'm going to help keep earth clean. Are you?

Because of hunters and farmers, tigers are becoming very rare. They now live only on special reserves.

Keep Your Environment Healthy

▶ Do not throw litter (trash) on the ground or in the water.
▶ Turn off lights when you are not using them.
▶ Do not leave the water running.
▶ Recycle.

Types of Pollution and Their Causes

1. Air pollution: car exhaust, cigarettes
2. Noise pollution: airplanes, stereos, TV
3. Water pollution: toxic waste, bug spray
4. Land pollution: litter, garbage

Recycling is changing products so they can be used again.

Air pollution can make it harder to breathe. Air pollution can also cause asthma attacks for people who have asthma. Do you know what asthma is?

 Why did the man pour vegetables all over the world?

35

Believe It or Not

Lucky Cody. His birthday is next week.
He wants a supersonic rocket that he saw on TV.
Sometimes things look better on TV than they
really are.
At least that is what Dad says.

I think Dad is right.

I saw some sparkly purple
soap on TV.
Mom let me buy some
with my allowance.
It cost two whole dollars!

I was going to take a bath
every day!
But the bubbles stuck to
the tub and made a mess.
Cleaning up a purple bathtub
is not fun. It wasn't even that
sparkly.

Mom wouldn't let me give
it to Cody for his birthday.

**An advertisement is some-
thing that tries to sell you a
product. Should you believe
all advertisements?**

Don't Be a Mouse Potato!

Instead of watching TV, playing video games, or sitting
at a computer, you can . . .

▶ Play basketball or baseball
  with your family or a friend.

▶ Help your family or a
  neighbor do yard work.

▶ Roll down a hill.

▶ Clean the garage or
  bathtub.

▶ Count how many ways you
  can stretch or move your
  body.

▶ Go for a hike with your
  family!

36

Verb Day!

Guess what!
Today is the last day
of school.
It's called Verb Day!
Do you know what a **verb** is?

The fifth graders set up verb
stations on the playground.
Verb stations are posters that
give us different verbs to do.
Some verb stations had easy
verbs, like dance, flop, and
leap.

Other stations had verbs like dodge, twist, and whirl.

If you could make up a verb station, what would it say?

At the end of the day, Ms. Ling asked us what verbs we were going to do during summer vacation.

I said I was going to splash, paddle, and dive.
What do you think I'm going to do this summer?
I'll give you a hint. It's wet.

Maybe I'll get a dog this summer too.
Then I can walk, pet, and hug my dog every day.
I wish I had a dog.

Neka said she's going to flip, roll, and tumble.
What do you think Neka is going to do this summer?

I sure did learn a bunch of fun stuff this year.
I hope you did too.

What big surprise was waiting for Ruby at the end of the last day of school?

Verbs!

▶ Pounce like a panther.
▶ Trot like a pony.
▶ Scurry like a mouse.
▶ Soar like an eagle.

What verbs are you going to do this summer?

Riddle Answers

The numbers match the lesson numbers in the text.

Unit 1 Answers

4. What do cows do after an earthquake? Make milkshakes.

9. How do baby fish swim? They do the crawl.

Unit 2 Answers

15. Why did the orange stop? Because she ran out of juice.

Unit 3 Answers

18. What does a moose get when he lifts weights? Moosles.

19. What part of your body has the most rhythm? Your eardrums.

21. What did the pony tell the doctor when she had a sore throat? "I'm a little hoarse."

Unit 4 Answers

25. What clothing does a house wear? Address.

Unit 5 Answers

31. What are the most common letters in the skunk alphabet? P and U.

Unit 6 Answers

34. Why did the man pour vegetables all over the world? Because he wanted peas on earth.